Dear Joe & Phyllis,

In absentia, still good friends.

I think of you often.

Ron Gillette

Hardware & Variety

Ronald Gillette

Some of these poems have appeared
in the following books and periodicals:

Lucky Star:	Singing in Place
	The Death of Jazz in the Soviet Union
	Black Sky Blues
Open Stock:	Apology
	Follow at a Distance
	The Sweet Song of Nothing
	That is Not Itself
	Luggage
New Souls, New Poems:	Authoress
Chicago Review:	Mirages of the Flying Bacon
Passages:	Flatlands
	The Hunt
Kettlestrings:	Rising to the Occasion
	on the Banks of the DesPlaines
	Nomad Frame
	Her Vision of the Cause
Gone Soft:	Beanery Walls Not Containing

First Edition

A one-hour cassette of selections from this book, read by the author, is available from the Erie Street Press, 221 South Clinton, Oak Park, IL 60302. Send $5.00 plus 75 cents for mailing. Allow six weeks for delivery.

ISBN 0-942582-07-1

The Erie Street Press, 221 South Clinton, Oak Park, IL 60302

Printed in the United States of America

WHAT'S GOING ON

I started writing poetry at 16, inspired by a high school friend's Spoon Riverish interpretations of our classmates. Those poems, so close to home, so full of the author's loves, hates, bemusements, and boredoms, *mattered* to me--- the first poems that did. Previously, I hadn't imagined that poetry could be clear, enjoyable, or written by one who walked among us. Sandburg, Frost, Williams, Stevens, Cummings, Eliot, Pound, and Ogden Nash were still alive, but I, like most people, assumed that death was prerequisite to being a poet--- death and some sort of degree.

But, if my friend could use the sounds and shapes of language to create some heat and shed some light, so, I thought, could I. I began trying. Fortunately, my critical powers were as weak as my poetic powers, so each flush-left, ragged-right batch of words (was all they were) pleased me and inspired another go.

Seven years and hundreds of poems later, some improvement was noticeable. Three poems in this collection are massive revisions of poems sketched that year (1967). Six poems here were written in 1984, after an additional 17 years of writing that I hope and do believe has grown decreasingly bad. (One *can* grow decreasingly!)

Practice, contact with other poets' work, and accumulation of life experience get credit for any decrease. I'd also like to credit a book, *Old Snow Just Melting* (University of Michigan Press, Ann Arbor), a compilation of Marvin Bell essays and interviews on poetics. If my poems don't show signs of that influence, it's only because there isn't enough truth in the old saw that "Whatever one can conceive and believe, he can achieve."

I offer this history as a partial explanation for the lack of stated organization here. It doesn't seem right to arrange 24 years of slow maturation chronologically or thematically. So, only occasionally does a pair of poems appear side by side for comparison, contrast, or contradiction. Readers who appreciate knowing what a poet ate for (I) Breakfast, (II) Lunch, and (III) Dinner may not sit comfortably at this table. The hardware of the title isn't grouped in aisle six behind the barrette rack.

I won't state the book's organization, but I'll try to illuminate its *dis*organization: At no point in my writing have I thought of myself as being a member of a school. I'm not an angry poet, a happy poet, a poet of the surreal, the mundane, the erotic, or the ethereal. Only individual poems fit into those categories, and then, usually, imperfectly.

If this book is *about* something, it seems to me to be about fitting or not fitting with one's circumstances--- settling down comfortably or uncomfortably, running away literally or figuratively, exploding, imploding, simmering, or saying Om. And, as I have no particular confidence in any of those solutions, I've attempted to scatter them among each other.

That scatter, by the way, is the only autobiographical aspect of this collection. I've never looked like Liz Taylor, I did not meet Dylan Thomas, and I'm not considering suicide.

I am going to do more writing, contact more poets, and accumulate more experience. For now, though, this collection contains my best work.

Donald Gillette
1984

To Ann, Meghan, and Jason

CONTENTS

Hardware & Variety

**Ronald
Gillette**

INVESTIGATOR

Is it real?
Is it true?
Is it good?
These are random
questions you ask
as if searching a coat
that's hanging on a rack.
But *you* are the rack
the coat was made for.
You put on the coat
and all its pockets
and, back on the street,
you button up tight.

SINGING IN PLACE

Visitors laugh at our emphasis on lawns.
No lotuses here, they say. They are wrong.
Jazz, for those who listen,
pours from squabbling children,
the rattle of trash on its way;
there's dance in the delivery of mail, in parking,
and plastic arts in the all-night pantry.
Meditation, really, is as deeply done
on asphalt as raked sand.

Screaming of chaos or coffee break,
a pair of copcars tears through our tunnel
of maples, and neighbors
are helicopter seeds pulled in swirls on porches.
What happened? What happened?

And when that dies---
when the Loch Ness head of an actual event
goes back to its sleep in black water,
the street, we notice, is in need of repair---
the porches, the brooms---
and only a few of the helicopters land
in soil that receives them
deeply enough. *That* deeply.
But all places are the same.
Seed is always struggling.

Underground, the trees send their passion forth
to penetrate our virginal garage floors and sewers.
O, outraged father, does no part of you
admire that zeal?
You and the prairie that was here before you
are partners in this
unlikely business of owning land.
To have fenced off a square! A square of what?

The earth goes on, and animals galore
have no *concept* of being stray.
Insurance and contracts blow away.
Your tree roots nudge through the illusion.
This is *not your yard!*
The dock, the thistles, goldenrod and plantain
will dance on your imperialist grave.

The *dream* you had ---of *being* a tree root ---
was real. You are not an ax.
You must move slowly against the obstacles
away from TV. (No, jingles aren't poems.)

Here is a poem: Our families as we dreamt them,
as they *might* be. Our families,
rooting in each other, in themselves,
as insistent as trees to crack up concrete.
Concrete, though, is powerful stuff. Even now,
an inhuman icing is forming over
what we know was once cake.

To bike through a swarm of invisible flies
is to know with one's face
what went wrong with the vision:
Money and duty and ailments and setbacks
and diversion into worthy and unworthy realms.
The cyclists turn *the wrong way* into trees.

The mayor, in his way, is aware of this.
He is, in other words, *un*aware.
At the hall, he gets a call
from his wife, who wants bread.
On his way, will he get a loaf? Grudgingly.
The sewers are breaking! *That's* his concern!
His workload is breaking his back, his heart
is not in it, the sewers, the loaf.

"There is trash and squabbling in the jazz, you mean."
Is there salt in the water or water in the salt
of such tears? Or is this a sea of joy?
There is sculpture in the birdbaths
and jockeys and flamingos.
The giant lumberjack looks over us all.

Can he see beyond The Dells, Las Vegas, or Heaven?
Farther than a carful of boys just out of high school
scouring a spring night to the county line
for the origin of a searchlight,
the future of themselves?
A snootful of that adolescent air may fuel escape!
Can a wooden figure see that far
or only to the fireballs that fall to earth
where they began
to ponder the freight tracks out of town
and the carnies that blow in
versus work at Wards?
To know the merchandise intimately
is something solid,
but the memory of that night
is something else. There is this in that.
Stan rings up a sale on chain-link fencing
as the night reasserts a *bigger* America.
Gas stations whiz past, and Bob and Ernie
lean out and holler at a girl in purple stretchpants.
She is all the world they have never seen.
Thank you, thank you.
Thanks for shopping Wards,

ladies and gentlemen sitting on the stoop,
as the breeze that follows twilight
rings the curtain down,
there is drama, surely, in the reverie—
in the self-satisfaction, such as it is:

14

"Mother, we've done well. Or *would* have done *if.*"
. . . in the hunger that remains, such as *it* is:
Iced tea sweats and cigarette smoke curls
blue into black, disappearing to the moon.
"Mother, well, . . ." and, "Well, . . . " dad says
under mercury lights and moths.
Howie Newsome and some of his pals
roll some joints in the cemetery.
"Wanna head to da mall an' see what's happening?"

But not even at the mall
can one see what is happening.
In a short time, all the lights go out
and nothing is happening here but dreams.

And again a little while and ye *shall* see

squirrels!—As illuminating as anything else.
Heedless of their image at 6am, they are at their best,
tearing all over the sleeping suburb
like pink crepe paper at a birthday party,
giggling in Chinese their be-bop.
That game of tag predates these houses
and any gears that move these neighbors
by thousands of years---a precedent for
the survival of the squirreliest.
Temporary shelters and resilient squirrels
and a mayor and trees and cars and kids . . .
If there are no lotuses here, I will eat
this fast food and go on,
with the squirrels,
unquestioning!
There is art in life.

BEANERY WALLS NOT CONTAINING

What is a ten-cent cigar to him?
A way of face, but more important,
a chance to dime her hand
(sparkleap on otherwise dry days),
touch and receive touch.
Fiddle with the gold band while puffing.

He slouches over chili like the next man.
She sees no more love in his spoon
than in *a* spoon.
She smiles, a cordial waitress
not knowing

What belief he has in Home Cookin'!
and that he would order pie
in that imagined home
and would be a

daily customer,
tipping through the years.
"Ralph," she calls him,
polishing the counter.
. . . would be ordering sweet berries if she . . .

Yet containing.

She hands him the newspaper
and he reads.

VICTORY FIRES

Gold and brown fur and wool
now have bound the coed flesh
on the 50-yard line.
She is halfway here, halfway there,
like the gold and brown leaves.

But beneath the school colors, her
field's hot cider, later to be drunk
with a man chosen from the gridiron engines—
a man roaring CONTEST even when he's finished
hooving rough the partially frozen sod.

Is it secretly for cider that confetti flies?
Yes. That nip in the air
is a sexual nip despite the cold teeth.
Magnetic flesh is the game's momentum
and it will not stop.

Each fan bellows victory fires.
The fleshteam wins!
The blooming will go on!
Their breathing becomes confetti
at the scoring of one goal.

THE HUNT

The zealot's focus, leonine,
blazed in lion hunters' eyes
when tall grass twitched
in ways they knew
it would not move without good reason.
Rising slowly from camouflaged chairs,
they padded
with tense ease learned from
the objects of their need
to triggers of cameras, cages, guns—
to triggers of whatever
they thought could capture
what they thought they loved
about the lion.
That, of course, is one way to mark
kinds of love that move in the jungle.

Monkey hunters watched the trees
for relevance of movement there:
A straight-growing limb
meaningfully bent
signalled the nearness of *their* requital.
If glide replaced frolic in the trees,
snake hunters flickered,
uncoiled, tumesced.
After elephant, insect, vegetation,
hunters were moved.
How many kinds of prey were moving?
Another widespread way of counting
kinds of love that move in the jungle

or in the village where a back-slung babe
plotted ways to find
the nuzzle of food;
or in downtown Urbania, where Mowgli's lust
produced incendiary bombs

that blew his rivals out of power,
or in the hut of the maker of drums,
where single-minded fury honed
an instrument to summon gods.
The prey, the food, the power, the glory,
and all the needs we hunted then
were born on the run.
So we pursued.
And were eluded.

We thrashed the bloody dither
till the green was down
and captured only a desperate guess:
There *is* no love that moves in the jungle.
There is no love that *needs* to move.
Needless, immobile, that mythical beast,
in all-but-invisible quietude,
cannot be hunted.
It can only be found, the theory ran.

RISING TO THE OCCASION
ON THE BANKS OF THE DESPLAINES

The dream of pioneers is rare
but recurrent. It's a test
that'll pass if one's pillow is fluffed.
Some fluff it.
But others welcome gristle.
They listen to rivers churn
whatever they contain.
Now, *this* river churns a lot of scum, but,
always on the way to finding new blood,
it isn't dead. It carries baptism
to those who enlarge
their scout knives to *carve*.
This river this spring
rose to such a level.

Folks awoke when they heard the water rising.
They scuttled from their suburbs
past the Tastee Freeze.
"Wouldja lookit that!" they said, and did.
And skimmed stones and boated and some fell in.

And two disappeared at Dam Number 4.
Newspapers called it "the dam of death."
The water was still rising,
the newspapers were rising,
and the folks with the firehats
in the backs of their closets---
O, boy! Did they rise!
Than longen folk to goon on pilgrimages!
Hey, shovels! Ho, flashlights! Bobby, get a rope!

But this crowd assembled for serious purpose:
Two people are missing. They're probably dead.
The community that came out here
knows there's not much chance of doing more

than finding proof; but, *besides* that,
struggles toward serious purpose.

Roger walks into the woods.
Channel 2 films three guys
tying ropes to a tree
and sandwiches being handed out.
Somebody goes to the hardware store.
For what? a team captain wants to know---
"The fire department has loaned us equipment."

Long-faced, apologetic,
they will hand the victims' families
the muddy lumps,
thinking, "Just like on TV."

At a jutty, Will and Kevin shout, "Over here!"
but it turns out there are no bodies there.

Suburbanites live outside the vital core
and this adventure makes them giddy.
This life-and-death stuff is too new to be faced
head-on; the rescuers are headed off.
There's a growing sense of picnic.
There's running and shouting and rushing water;
new hipboots, bought for the day,
and the proliferating green of the forest preserve.
But this is *not just* another picnic.
The underwater duet keeps singing the sackracers
heavy questions: "Where are we? Who are you?"

Roger comes back. "I took a leak,"
he tells Channel 7, and then feels dumb.
Those words may be his last to a microphone.
He goes back to searching with all his might.
Even the divers share his fear.
They're afraid they'll miss the big events,
and each hopes he'll be able to give his wife
a firsthand account: "It was terrible! Just terrible!"

Upriver, a boy in a boat hears the sounds of spring
that are rising and rising. He rows to the dam.
The action of the water is irresistable.
Off-camera, but in the thick of things, he goes down.

"I saw him go down," a witness offers.
One of the first two victims is found.
"Two take away one . . . plus one . . . is two,"
the scoutmaster thinks. His back is sore.
"Where's Roger?" one of his buddies asks.
One of the scoutmaster's buddies? No.

Fifty million dollars in stolen bonds
turns up. They are public improvement
bonds for Houston, stolen last year from a printing firm.
Reporters on the scene swing into action
and scuba director Beardsley has a fatal heart attack.
Becoming victim number . . . ?

"Rosemont's death dam claimed two more lives *but*
yielded fifty million dollars,"
Bill Griffin wrote in the Sunday Tribune,
hinting at something like fair exchange.

Riverwater, sweat, and beer--- the scorecard is wet.
"Where do we stand?" ask the lost and found.

Sobieski has new arms. The old ones weren't
as strong as these.
"Where do we stand?" ask the lost and found.
Martens now knows he'd rather garden.
"Where do we stand?" ask the lost and found.
"They don't follow orders," a sergeant gripes.
"I saw him go down," a witness recalls.
"Wouldja lookit that!"
"It was terrible!"

And George is dead and Terri is dead
and Ron is dead and Jessie is dead
and something in Ed Stiegler died:
"I'm not Jacques Cousteau," he realizes,
and is reborn understanding himself
as someone else. Where do we stand?

One of the unidentified victims is claimed by his wife
who knows for sure his constellation of warts.
Another is known by the company he keeps,
a third, for his pleasant manner.
By their works, ye may or may not be able
to know the survivors as they are at this moment.
But ole man river, he just keeps rising
and rising to occasions such as this day.
And rising and returning to rollin' along.

Where do we stand?
O, *more* than fifty million ahead.

MINIMALISTS IN LOVE

We'd collected twigs (the scratchiest), rocks, and dirt.
Tan, white, gray, rust, olive, umber, black:
Those were the colors we invested with power.
In the afternoon, we sat in the den, and over coffee,
watched a light rain haze the naked wood.
And now, we remember, though we do not speak.

AUTHORESS

fire batons untwirled,
waiting for her days to mean more
intelligible sparks
and compel the written keg to voluminous movements,
knowing, while waiting,
that meat-space punctuation twitches
through burning beings
that spark in choppy syllables,

she sails.
head thrown back in free laugh slaps
(as young girls sometimes throw their heads),
she speeds away from knotty pages
trailing her fire batons in brine
(the glory of long, wet hair
that feels against one's cheek
and a few strands in her mouth).

before we were married, he insists,
you wrote like the fiery artist you are.
when was the last time you wrote a page?
but she is stubborn
(despite Master's degree)
and does not produce, saying,
writing is more than parts of speech.
and other excuses.

she sews.
knitting her brows,
an irregular stitch across her forehead
binds concentration's fabric tight
until a needle pricks her finger
into her mouth.
a drop of blood, a squeal, a suck,
a laugh, a joke about clumsiness.

parts of speech! he misses the point,
I'm speaking of content! I'm speaking of style!
you have so much more than craft!
she hums while the mailman
is watched up the walk,
hums while the potroast
roasts, then says,
I'm out of ideas.

in November, on horseback,
she pretended to be royal---
heard the hounds and watched for foxes.
none appeared.
the queen was forced to be content
with autumn, wooden fences, farms---
nothing more than even commoners
can have.

from me to you, he smiles---
a ream of inspiration.
fresh white sheets
are full of ideas.
spend some time every night
and before you know it . . .
why not try a mystery?
you used to have that form down cold.

The Case (she twirls her batons
in a very private way)
of the Vanishing Period---
last seen about a month ago.
she smiles
at her breasts now just a little swollen.
out of bed early mornings,
she tries to vomit proof.

internal fire batons are twirling!
under the dinner table,
her lap
and the busy gurgle of her best idea.
and when he asks her what she's written
today she reads
a list of male names
and a list of female.

choosing prospective characters' names?
yes.
then laughter until he understands---
until he knows, while waiting,
that meat-space punctuation twitches
through burning beings
that spark in choppy syllables
called living.

SECRETING REEDS

You allowed a serpentine woodwind to enter
your inner ear, deposit a bead of oriental oil.
You wove a nest of your most minute hairs
and there the bead set, became
a perfect black pearl, a round secret to finger
during even your blandest public agenda.

MIRAGES OF THE FLYING BACON

It is midsummer.
Of an afternoon, in a field of newmown grass,
I am unstable. I am the bacon.
My grease rises in green vapor
seeking meaning in salt
and pork beyond the dream heater
(this summer afternoon, the white sky).

I, the frying, flying bacon
sizzle a dance of distant pigs
(dem smokehouse blues!);
the salt wind chafing ancient sailors' faces
as they shade their eyes to watch me pass above the rigging.
"I am the fat! I am the lean!
The universe is in my image
when I fry in the griddle grass!" I call to them.
They are surprised to hear such words
from one not dressed in summer whites.

Despite the blinding sky, I see
baconness is everywhere.
I thank the summer grass for sails, heat for catalyzing dream.
For what is bacon without fancy?
Born to blister at cooks' whims, the bacon is, at best,
a side dish cut from swine.

THE GOODBYE ROOM

Never was a break
less clean. She left
the room
in which this may have happened:
I was young, she was twenty-seven.

Perfumed and Sad at the absence of
an earlier love, she did not speak
of her love of me directly
but opened to me
the room of herself,
a room so apart from
my circumstantial traffic,
windburns and acids
that I knew she'd been similarly
disaffected.
I felt in that room
the place left for me.

Sad at her Sadness
and my cumbersome newness,
I didn't speak directly
of my fantasies of her.
But she showed me her hair
in confidential curlers!
Concerns disappeared
in her dressing gown.
(Silken gold, golden silk, oriental greens,
o, not spun on domestic machines!)
But if it was, what of it?

But Sad? O, we were!
We held and gulped each other's
breaths to keep our haven,
find a not-so-Sad.
Our bodies strained to feel

the abandon of the land
of shampoo commercials--- O, pastorale!

But *the room!*
The room!
That wine was sure wine,
and Mozart was Mozart!
The threadbare rug, the booklined wall,
the kisses, crying, perfume,
new and not-so-new
were too set a set to ever set us free
that year.
For one of us to go, a phantom'd have to've whispered
in her heart, "h o r i z o n !"

She faded. I kissed
her hands and carried her
down to her car.
Mozart by perfume by dressing gown,
the room was bled white,
went blind in the light of an incidental street.
I even carried curlers, I imagine, in one box.

We cried final autumn (The trees were perfect!)
and the rest was carbon monoxide and dust.

I blamed the car, I blamed the room,
I blamed inexperience,
but, gradually, I entered the buzzing minutiae
I'd thought were insect life
by comparison to ours, so elevated.
And I became able to breathe on my own.

Now I blame only the window as I see it---
from the prosaic street (I guess it always was)
that black square is only
an opaque artifact left by a vanished
people---O, Sad!--- their magnificent illusions!

THE SWEET SONG OF NOTHING
THAT IS NOT ITSELF

Was there a summer in which I did nothing?
A summer in which locusts   were,
and, wistful, the unwashed dog and I
lay against each other, boneless as tongues
where spiders powdered on cool cement?

Clear from such a summer
is the low-pitched squeek of the growing oak
and "day" as I sighed it---as a faucet drips---
softly, to be vaporized
by noctiferous breezes.

When apples began their winey ebb,
actors gathered the brittle leaves that,
through a thousand colors, had turned brown.
And to brown smoke they turned them,
it joining the exhausted sky.

A cot that color on the screened-in porch.
Smoothly slid an oyster in an oblate gourmand,
his esophagus wet with its function.
That cot was as smooth--- not sad.
That autumn as autumnal as others.

If I here recall winter (blue television light
that leaked through stormwindows, whispered to snow)
and spring (the adolescent pores of the soil)
you'll imagine this a paean to the seasons,
but that's a weary lover.

In that marvelous fatigue,
cosmic endearments need no definition.
His voice, her smell are familiar, nothing.
And now there is time.
And now there is time.

APOLOGY

I've got to take credit for something like love
or a perverse spirit in this goddamn town
that turns my words in circles,
turns my visions to words.

I've got to take credit
for what may be my last
attractive folly --- something
like love for you mixed among my words.

Not *just* perversity led me away
from the boarded-up town of the academic argument ---
Certainly not a test case!
Certainly not a footnote!

This slope we're on, though, *has* to be windward
if I'm to rise above proving death rattle.
"Spavo! Spavo!" a sax wails in the distance.
It *must* be approaching if . . .

Help! The last innocence!

Well you may wonder if you've been fooled ---
if you're a lover to a twittering machine
that tells you it's been programmed for
"something like love."

FLATLANDS

She doesn't like the smell
of the room in which the batter
that's used to make the tires
is stored. She goes away.
She waits on the loading dock
(no one goes far), so little left
of her eyes to watch him
scatter sweeping compound,
feeding the last of
his invisible brood.
A metal door rolls down.

She saves for her shift
at the diner only
the strength to hoist chairs
to their tables for the night.
He settles his bulk
in the dark Dodge to wait
for the Coke light to go out,
for the gravel in the lot
to crunch.
But his eyes are almost gone.
He can hardly watch her now.
He and the birds of 4am
trade states.
When she does come, she does not
immediately poke him drive.

She rubs her legs,
for, here, considerations
of dawn are numb---
not jungle, not mountains,
but incessant wheat.
Rails and wires make a vanishing point.
Long ago, the local semaphor's wink
became slow,

became slower.
Boxcars detached.
Love, decay, geography, these two.
Here is a hailstone that fell last month.
Once she saw a movie that was larger than life.

AUDITION, DANSEUSE

"The floor was too slippery
to really *do* it.
I had to smile and present my arms."

"Did you sing with the singers?"
"No, I had to impress them
with my *talent*."

Her translucent forehead
is blue and pulsing,
indicating diagrams of brain and heart.

MOODBIRTH

on afternoons made brittle
by what were, after all,
internal events,
we burned incense.
literally, I mean, we burned
incense on muggy afternoons.
we blended dusky foreign perfumes
with air that required elaboration,
for it lay heavy
and provincial as a tomb
within us (as i said,
the intensified afternoons
took place largely
in our minds --- a droning).
our droning brown perfume
elaborated on the dead air and,
if any wind existed, it was ours,
and it moved clouds,
made gongs reverberate
in undulating waves through glass.
how could we but swim with those waves ---
those self-propelled currents
if they existed outside ourselves?
we swam with them
toward the less-glassy banks
of the stagnant sky.
we burned incense.

THE STUDENT FROG

Though efficient flypaper,
what a limited tongue tool glue is
for expressing the smell of an orrkit
or the heat of the wrrocks on which frogs sun!
What syrruppy wurrt is there
to describe the sun?

The green lump, for whom time and the sun
loll in the swamp like the slow oil of dinosaurs,
says, "Warp." Meaning sun?
As in afternoon heat above water?
Sun as it happens when fewer mosquitos are to be had?
"Warp. Warp."

There is no serviceable croak for "fireball"
until a boy from another world comes with his magnifying lens
and focuses one truth on dormant frog eloquence.
That truth is that glue has its place; so do muscles
that know without pause that
*boys*and*sun*can*reduce*frogness*to*an*ability*to*

leap into new concepts of frog, boy, sun
and the interrelation of the three,
blister avoidance.
Though newborn, this new understanding
is well defined and muscled by
one lesson.

THE NATURE OF NATURE

Nature's vivid colors can heighten,
possibly even inspire emotions.
Its extreme contrasts in size can move
the most unimaginative person to ponder
his or her place in the "scheme" of things.

When nature hurts or breaks something of value,
we call nature cruel or violent
though most of its grossest destruction also creates.
We read in volition and want revenge.
The truth is that nature does what it must
or, worse, that it's only an accident.

None of this is pleasant, but less pleasant still
is our problem of being and not being part of
what we mean when we say nature.
Is nature what is? Or distinct from "only human"?

This poem--- its writing--- was a natural act
and is therefore neither good or bad,
but it was easy to write because it does not speak
of human relationships (except the one
of humans to nature (assuming humans are something other,
in which case the poem discusses nature's relationship
to nature). This stanza was the hardest one so far.

Many words that describe nature are very evocative,
but this poem does not contain many such words,
This is a poem of big ideas.
"Moonlight," "windward," and "alluvial plain"
are words that give a lot of pleasure---
more than "relationships" which I used last stanza.
If you are a weak poet, include such words
and you'll thrill more than a few readers
and even more listeners as they fill in your blanks.
That's natural.

Some people claim that nature belongs in rural areas---
that there is no nature in big cities.
This is wrong. There are pigeons there.

Nature should probably require, always,
a capital N, because it is such a big concept.
It is so big that even people
who cannot identify more than two or three
kinds of trees attempt to discuss it,
explain it, as even I am doing.
Perhaps I haven't done a very good job,
but I'd rather have been writing
about how unhappy I am to be so unloved.

"There isn't a bit of truth in your poem!" my wife said.
"I suppose *you* could do better," I said.
It took her about 15 minutes to write

> *Husband, the smell of fallen fruit*
> *may mark an ending.*
> *There is no doubt that a pie that flavor*
> *would end your love of pie.*
> *Nor is there doubt that this year's yield*
> *can now be tallied.*
>
> *In years to come, though,*
> *when our eyes are closed and ears distracted,*
> *this afternoon may re-enter our hearts*
> *through our primitive sense,*
> *through apples that recall*
> *how their ancestors died.*

Not bad for someone who isn't a poet,
but it's not my style
and it misses the bigness of the concept of nature.
Perhaps even *my* poem is somewhat deficient.
My best poems are about how unloved I am.

POOLSIDE BRUNCH

We have worked hard
our women have worked hard
to earn our ways next to
this shimmering turquoise
to breath its light
chlorine assurance
that the world can be purified.

Now we deserve
the cooling effect
its evaporation has
on our bedwarm skins
for the day may turn hot
and we have worked hard
and our grandfathers worked hard.

Soon our women
will come out.
But our patience, too,
may soon run out —
the juice — too warm —
an irritation.
In contrast, as it should be,
dependably folded on a wicker chair,
a newspaper, with *REVOLUCION* very deeply buried
on an inside fold.
But a fold that some mongrel, some cur has chewed
in an effort to deprive the paper's rightful owner
through insupportable, irrational, violent behavior,
an antisocial act — the snatching away
of the news of the day,
GOLD SOARS on top.

Absently, I push
my cuticles back
with my gold letter opener.

I won't guess what you heard
last night outside the wall.
"A lizard dies a senseless death,"
I say. We have worked hard.

But our women are here,
exquisite as they pass
the breeze-rippled blue.
Their images break and recombine
with the sun and the cabaña
in a cubist mosaic.
"Nothing is too good for them," I repeat.

IT SAID WE ARE HAUNTED

The news is piped in: Someone's been hit!
A ghost tells a story of ghosts in Khartoum
and guesses at what we should feel about it.
But we have no substance. We are out of earshot.
We are watching dental cream. We are watching our steps.
We go sit on the stoop. The air is full of impulses.

THE ELEPHANT

"Ich sehe dass wir Nichts *wissen können.*
Dass will mich schier das Herz verbrennen."

Goethe's *Faust*

(1)

Leaves among leaves turn to light, turn to leaves,
and simple animals smell their ways.
They cast their own shadows---
the shadows of animals,
the shadows of leaves.

And I, when I was motile jelly,
moved as motile jelly in saline ambience.
Those times gone by.
Higher forms.

(2)

Five blind men feel
something's gone wrong.
Fingers pressed to foreheads,
each matter is gray,
immense, beyond them.

"Rope," says the man who makes connections
but is tightly bound, an immobile bundle.
"Snake," says the one who sheds his skin
only to find another takes its place.

The man who feels the tree
feels concentric rings encasing his heart,
can do the trick of seeming to be dead
when the world ices over.

Mystified by that is the man who feels the leaf.

He is so thin he cannot imagine
stoic resistance to a blast of white,
cannot imagine at the fringes he inhabits
the thickness of a trunk, the thrust of a root.
He feels he
can hang on just so long.

Number five and we all
know about a wall.
We have watched mimes pat it
seeking entry or escape.

Entry or escape. But each animal and leaf
goes its way without us;
we, without them.
We without or within ourselves,

touching the gray barrier.

(3)

At 20 you noticed summer
again had granted
hometown trees their ability to whisper
coded instructions you could not follow.
You could not get closer to
trees or yourself
nor interpret the pain.

Nor did the elephant.

Much sweetness was clear.
The matted grass, the warm population,
known words that would be spoken next.
Cloud shapes repeated over and over your
home and the so-familiar trees

seemed poised to reveal
your missing self --- that elusive germ-plasm
that might have lulled you on needle nights
or powered a drive for adulthood, completeness.

Do you now believe it hid in the trees
that summer night so long ago?
Perhaps the red eyes of the elephant shifted
up to sort the leaves so imperceptibly
that you did not perceive it.

Your senses were nestled in a molecule
in which street names had acquired power.
Too young for real descant, you repeated them
and found a possession lost ten years:
Your possession, glee, grass, pencil,
mother, father, friends, porch, shoes, bed, fence,
and *your* discomfort and separation
from these, from your griefs, from your exultations,
your body, mind, spirit, and outside world.

Even that Orion then
flowed with family blood ---
a cosmic uncle who guarded snowmen ---
an uncle with a magic watch
who's now only stars
which are only gas
very far away.

Do you now believe it hid in the stars
that winter night so long ago?
What now hides stars and is large and gray,
close and stultifying?

(4)

If circumstance takes you, a jar from the shelf,
to local breezes that stir incense bells,
you'll still be unsure one sky covers all.

42

How alien is the ball on which you stand!
How alien is your state of dream!

Are you the brown couple, wet with each other
as bone beads rattle and green birds sleep?
The legless thief? His serpentine knife?
The mosaic in its handle? An undulating rope?

The elephant, on its ancient pillars,
does not move toward you or away.
It is integral, like the air;
environment, not invention,
and here takes the form of veils and pushcarts.

(5)

Zack puts Corn Huskers on his raw hands
and goes on the porch to ponder the elephant.
It's purple in the twilight
and the newly purchased combine
seems a kin of sorts (though mechanical and green).
An hour to be enjoyed, and the fireflies

But the elephant.

And sometimes he pines for
a less lonely state
than Nebraska and wonders
why the big green investment
yonder don't fix it.

The elephant is like a barn, he thinks.
And as noncommittal
but commodious and quiet
but a duststorm and smells
of provender and decay
sometimes full, sometimes empty,
especially now that the family's gone.

(6)

Also down neon-fried streets you chase
electric depictions of bare-assed excess,
wire food, pill food, hair on fire
and close no distance.
Awright, you hit a tempo, but bleary now and straining
mechanically down a funnel and close no distance,
the elephant steadfastly gray,

standing at the jetport, blinking, not moving.
Staggering tourists win and lose,
but the elephant remains
barrier and pain.
Stands, a planet of muscle and pulse that does not here
say anything.

From motiveless caves long ago swam up
those constant red fish to the surface of that
. . . brain?
to blink and blink, neither portent nor promise.
Just the click of two pebbles on elephant mountain.

(7)

Palpable fragments of the city, 6 am:
If Bingo hears the fat bundle of newsprint
hit the walk, it makes a sound. The van growls onward.
Waddling, hatblind, scowling underneath,
he squats to cut ties, begin building a display.
"Ah doan ass kwetchuns. Ah doan ass no kwetchuns,"
his mutter of the day

has not begun.
Two degrees below
the horizon and groaning,
the sun considers the what-color sky

and moves a minute.
This is a good time to squeegee windows.
Now start the day's first percolations.

Dave imagines he is a mahout
prodding the leaden, wrinkled bulk
of his truck through the jungle of loading docks.
It lumbers too close to the redbrick and
metal imitates that distinctive shriek
that warns the tropics of rage or fear.
Pigeons scatter and a super shakes his fist.

Dave, oh Dave! Your beast of burden
is not the elephant.
Your burden of beast stands silent between
you and your wife, your self, your truck.
It stands between you and the end of all alleys.

What are we doing awake at this hour
asleep at the wheel?

Then, four million people come.
Between each pair, an elephant,
within each skin.

(8)

We circle the fire and each of us glows.
Each face reflects,
seems to *be* the throbbing light.
But, of another world,
we cannot hold the gorgeous embers.
We touch them with twigs of wonder and fear
and our need for heat. We peek at consummation
from behind the elephant.
How, at any moment, can we know the juju?
How, at any moment, can we be?

How now, my wife, my daughter, my son?
How? I ask poets and primitive tribes,
astronomers and jazz musicians.
How? I ask the crying children.

A crying child says sincerely,
"The only one who loves me is my dog."
How now, brown cow?
How now, bacillus, inanimate object?
What do you think?

My circle of friends, circling, circling;
the river that flows to New Orleans,
past St. Louis, city of mystery
(why does it exist?)
and Hannibal, Missouri,
its thousands of mysteries,

and even my palm --- what can it do
with chemistry or electric impulses?
Weighed after death, will there be a difference
that will reveal the elephant departed?
How then?

For now, it is too rare and brief
being or escaping the animal
to whom maybe God or civilization,
genes or time gave tons of awareness
squeezed in the space of a pair of fists.

FACING UP TO THE JUNGLE

Cool evening air dives from Montortanji
and across the simmering lake it rushes.
We move our cots and a lamp to the porch.
Phillippe will smoke and I will talk
or Phillippe will talk and I will smoke
and insects whirr and dark fronds rustle
as if to say *Oalla wahzhizi*--- be asleep.
Asleep while waterlegs skate on the lake
and infinitessimal dents their pads make
catch moonlight as if they were tiny cups.

How easy it is for this pearlescent world
to encroach on any meaning! Perhaps tonight
a shower of meteors, a hint of metaphor,
a celebration on an impossible liner.
Pyrotechnics crackle over our lagoon and
corks pop fizz over captain's table and paper hats.
I tire of artifice. "What *is* this, Phillippe?"
I now will ask. And now erase Phillippe,
chosen for his name. So was Montortanji.
And what the hell is a waterleg?

Diversionary places will crop up
in the mind, the heart, or another seat of fancy,
peopled with exotics who move as they're told.
Home is March snow that returns to the sewers,
October leaves hurtling toward next year's mulch,
and *still* we run away to poeticize. As if to say,
Giveth and taketh away are one. Verily, I give you
a 7-11 in Schiller Park. Jack moves the Drumsticks
(those nut covered cones) to the back of the freezer
to catch the breeze from Montortanji. *Oalla wahzhizi!*

A LITTLE BIRD

I've always loved peewee
the word itself so much itself
so little. Privacy near secrecy
you need to coax the bird it is
appear. I may have had a
glimpse just then or thought
some hint of beak or feather
moved. An intimate setscrew.

For explaining P in an alphabet
the pelican's immodest bulk
and public swoop is only fast,
The Avian Award and we'll all be rich!
P is for poet who smells a fish.
The birth of a stork is only a joke
of form. The function of explaining
P's important, takes much time.

Put your ear to perforated mud
and at one pore your minute hairs
may pick up song, think, "Singing mud?"
The problem of life is not a problem
except as it's brayed by a speedy crowd
that never saw or heard a thing so small,
a note heart-breaking in exactitude:
peewee.   peewee.   But slower that that.

NOMAD FRAME

As the last slivers of night are lifted from what is to be,
nomads pause on a city's first hill
and with meticulous tweezers of their own
imagine cooks arising early,
clattering in the half-light
to re-establish the roots of their world---
the coffee, the bacon, the noise itself . . .
all proof that sleep has not erased the previous.

The sun begins to swell and throb.
The nomads walk among the shops
and the family members who, during the day,
are known by the labels of the jobs they hold.
The ads for the town touted local bees
as being the buzziest, but smiles and frowns and ups and downs
are second nature now to even bees,
and the town in its mediocre glory, says, "Sure."

The Friendly Shoemaker does a fast patch job
on a nomad shoe. He says outright he doubts it'll last
but is reassured that, good job or bad, his work will gain him
no repeat business. Without having made any guarantees,
the underfoot motion of the road
has trained its clients to dawn in the distance,
to borrow life like a smell of breakfast
that drifts beyond suburban hills.

STEERAGE

No choice of beverages on this raft, but,
arcing between horizons, there's plenty of one
an' it's plenty we've 'ad an' plenty we'll be 'avin'.
A toast: To ourselves, mates, a born race of navigators!
Lard, don't I see stars!
There, lads! That shade tree, floating above the surface!
We'll make for that and seventy years of drift.
Our masts need mates on this lonely voyage,
this dam-ned zigzag endless empty bloody fascination!
I seen them just now through my currently favorite sail.
Are we headin' toward that grove
                                      'at's me woman's laces
when we was fresh minted, her white veils, which was palms
what fringed the sand of a tropic coast and the silver moon
come up real slow. O, clever tars, we are steerin' somewheres!

O, we'll skim the top o' this water for now,
but when we get to the bottom o' this,
we'll see the low creatures what are slimy by nature
or slimy as slime has accrued down there
since they left this weathered deck---
our one-time mates, now fish-like or nothing.
"No time to look back" is our jolly song.
Our other songs are not our jolly song,
but no time to look back on our other songs.
Let's toast the brilliant flotsam with our only brew!

Let's go! On the wheel, our wondrous brown hands
made leather by the honor of the work we've done,
the decisions we've mustered on course and cause.
Make for that harbor there before it rises.
There! On that cloud, you lamebrains! A toast!

This vessel notes the hills we roll
by our wills, now up, now over, now down, and she rolls,
she rolls through nations of gill-breathers.

Underfoot don't you feel
the cargo shift
            to starboard, shift to port,

                        shifting as we guide the
            mainsail up the
                        deck, belay the mizzen the
                                    jib stern of a,
            the
sure hands hand the sure hand sure. They
            shift as we drift toward
our jolly song. O, white she was! A toast
to the suns, the storms, the Meridian! Harharharhar
harhar when I was a boy, we would not sleep away
nights such as these,
                        embroidered by islands,
                                    eventful as we
have decided they should be. We are sometimes jolly,
steering sure for
                that wave over there!! The one that we
measure in cubits or the
                        one in the mackintosh, Comrade Fish,
the one in the mackintosh, the one with

            the stereopticon. We steer there, don't we,

Mister Mast?   The rope is woven, rewoven, rewoven.
            The rope is woven, rewoven, rewoven.
And don't we drink jolly of our lot to be
                                    men free
                                            of the
strictures of
                        port--- the laws
                                    of this land or that?
The one with the
                        foam that boils backward!

Free men all, compasses true, hands leather, ship sure,
you miserable scum!

THE WEIGHTED CURTAIN

The shows
are over.
All of them.
Conceivers and enablers and performers all
and handlers of necessary paraphernalia
and sweepers up after
and the ones who turn off lights---
into this tent
and entertainment ceases.

"Are there lots of stars?"
ask the dimestore clerks,
grade school principals,
owners of carwashes.

Toothless, in his socks,
the man who most recently
has played God
recalls a snatch of script and says,
"There are those who are   ars
when the lighting allows
any glimmer,
when the box office vouches for
the grandiose.
But there is no show tonight
in this biggest of tents."

Outside, a giddy boy
auditions his Hamlet
to the warehouse of dummies.
Tomorrow, they may waken
and take him in,
but there is no show tonight
in this dusty, sighing respite.

"But, even in the dimestore
we have stars," says a clerk.
The face of the portrayer of God becomes a candle
and burns down.

Quality control in the kaleidoscope factory?
By a blind man, a farmer
who minds the drain
in the center of the tent---
a rice paddy wet by light and paint only,
which now swirl down to
the aquifiers of their minds.

On the way, the mix irrigates
the same dreams that silverware
lifts to the waitress,
the same dreams the busman drives:
Mother,
becoming,
becoming undone.
Rising,   falling,
falling,   rising,
breathing like a tent.
And the dreams themselves
are born and die
again and again in the home of collapse,
the biggest home.

We have put the bikes to sleep in the garage,
the dolly in her shoebox with the flannel scrap.
Goodnight illusions,
goodnight grip,
goodnight to the old lady whispering hush.
Goodnight stars.
Goodnight nobody.
In the great greenroom.

INVISIBLE SPECTRUM

green is brown in other places
in soil
in wood

and wood in weapons
is sometimes red.

the soil in Virginia's
a different red
and the Blue Ridge Mountains

curl unexpected time.
at first a subtle purple swims
royal into
blue it must be
8 pm.

later, when the purple
ought to have turned black,
electric toward the cities down the way

where blues ain't blues
riled riverbottom sky
as brown as the red of

the white amphetemine
gray turning black toward the end,

black returning green
after everything else.

in changing grass
a child on her back
letting clouds evolve
knows a wider spectrum
than a prism does

LUGGAGE

All of us
who can do no miracles
must, now
and then, rant our secular prayers
to those times when we were
(in retrospect)
holier.

In 1960 in New York with Jack?

"O, vanished comfterbles,
give me what I need now---
what I had in my greenery---
this day as it would have been then if
and there if and
if the departure
that's come to seem irrevocable
was mine, forgive.
Deliver me from
the photographs, scrapbooks,
letters and daydreams."

Or an hour alone on a farm?

The prayer answer's through
new land, time, and circumstance:
A favorite escape, the disappearance
of your troublesome god.

THE DEATH OF JAZZ IN THE SOVIET UNION

In the Union of Socialist Piano Bars
you *will* play reqvests, komrade!
Night Train one more time
and no kinky changes!
Blow for us now the solid party line---
oppressed Negroes working in Amerika
on the gang of chains.

Well, those gigs are always available,
and maybe you want for your wife a toaster
or yourself rise above ersatz see-gars.
Then byhebee, don't play revisionist!
You want relax for life at some cold Camarillo?
When they tell you chezz is happy music,
better smile, shuck and chive!

Believe or don't believe the official story
that chezz came up the Volga,
but many fine cats have gone up the river, sure!
Talk about after-hours cutting sessions!
Sergei got up on the stand at The Struggle
and found someone'd swiped his axe between sets.
That was the alto his uncle had carved!

These are dues you pay. You learn to stash
your bass in a poison ring, fold your trombone.
You play for crowds that are mostly red squares
the Tijuana Taxi and go home to wommit.
I know a drummer who has never played
on anything but practice pads!
But how do you take underground an alto?

In Amerika, is different. The state can send
Benny Goodman to Moscow, and always he goes home,
for, in Amerika, chezzmen are kings
and dukes and counts. The masses decide

what is not to listen to.
One trumpeter there has been so rewarded
he never has to wear the same clothes twice!

It makes me wonder (if this is true):
Do chezzmen in Amerika still get the blues?

FERTILITY AMUCK IN THE IMAGINATION

Cancerous romantics:
He stands waist-deep in semen;
she squats in the field, gives birth and works on,
  the new child sucking, sucking
  at her bulbous supply.
The air is more pollen than air,
  causing the already-laden bees
  to leer and drool.
The fenced-in stallion explodes,
  wet and snorting.

The real earth isn't fooled.
  Even calling it "earth"
  is some concession to the dreamers.
Some dirt is just no good.
  Some farmers know it;
  others don't, and die early.

But who's bitter?
  The wise rhythm of bad times
  makes the waterhole special.

EXPRESSWAY BY NIGHT

Of the ocean's metal, one opaque sheet
has accepted the moon and rolled out to cool.
The hairline is *not* a slice of the brain.
Many brave versions sleep in the deep.

You are looking for some penetration.
You are trying to drive home.
You ease into a school of chrome fish
and are caught in a stream of submarine bulk.
Caught in a lane near the school's collective spine,
you're dependent as an axon, precognate
until the last exit separates you from the others,
throws you back on your own
devices. Until then, you're a unit in this school.

But you *can* be other.
Which is to say, more.
Or, possibly, less.
Relax. Accustomed action
will guide your vacant body
until you return.

The spirit of your eyes can rise above the traffic.
As it does, the shim'ring trav'lers begin to scale down,
become a simple line and, finally, make sense.
Amid the many currents that have come into view,
you see the speck of self you left behind
pulsing through bright veins in a massive black body---
pulsing back to the omnipresent heart.

Penetration made, you splash down in time
to make the moves required
to extricate yourself.
On an overpass, you wonder
if you've *been* somewhere.

The calm of the surface
and the blinking polestar
assure you, "No, these are these ---
neither more nor fish."

TAILOR

He has the impression
that, in some sense,
his feet are stitching
a seam in the world.
So it's natural, he thinks,
that, when he swings those
world connectors
into his unconscious bed,
the world spins through space
and that he awakes disoriented,
an immigrant tailor,
ignorant of the local fashion.

The earth, unconcerned
with local fashion,
is not impressed.
Always it is spring "in some sense"
somewhere.
Somewhere's ripe for stitches.
Somewhere there are tailors.
Somewhere there's this one.
Goosh! He makes a point
in the vernal muck.

LULLABY

This land, this people cannot be tamed.
We have cleared the brush till there *is* no brush.
We've convinced submissive beasts to become stuffed toys
and caged or slaughtered the ruffians.
We've housebroken comets, nailed weather to the porch,
and erected serene billboards where once unruly nature was.
Things, we've decided, henceforth will be things.
Words, will be words, folks, folks. Etcetera.

But night comes and something gets at another farmhand
who carelessly has strayed too far from the barn.
A poet volunteers to look at what has happened.
He re-enacts the event for the whimpering survivors
as they huddle around the . . . *"YYEEARRH!"* the shaman reports.
His audience murmurs, keeping its distance.
"Perhaps it's this madman who's been tapping our blood,"
think his neighbors. They clutch their blood.

While leaping, while demonstrating how bone shatters,
while taking a piece of half-digested meat from his throat,
the shaman's mind wanders. " . . . aannd the ffarrmmmhaannd . . ."
He drifts into a song of love. "It melts environment," he sings,
"becomes a song of suction, twinges, manacles and warm dough.
Forever she is being too alive in me, too pain, too pain melting.
Even her consonantal names are mellifluous, inescapable
because I can't . . . I don't want . . . shall not . . . "

"Get back in here!" shouts Debbie from the edge of the ring.
She moves through the crowd, bearing new magic.
"Running around in your bare feet! Look at this mud!"
And the new magic captures the hill.
"Unga, bunga," say the natives, now daring to rise,
rising to adjust the color control,
controlling the control as if they *are* in control.
The farmhand, unnoticed, begins his long rot home.

"Dis is a nice couch," the shaman sez.
"Dat's nice," sez Debbie. "Jus' relax."
"Primed wit' malt brine, I can begin," he sez. "It's been a busy day."
"Beer
ain't brine," sez Debbie, "an' I don't see why you fool wit dat bunch.
Dey tink yer nuts, it tires you out
and dere's a lotta tings you could be doin' here---
Brush to clear, beasts to cage, . . . "

. . . comets to capture, billboards to build . . .
"*WAITAMINNIT!*" the shaman sez. "I'm trying to remember someting.
Primed wit' malt brine, I . . . I dunno."
He is trying to remember carnage and love
and hate and work and songs and fire
and the ability to remember.
And the feeling of being *really* primed.
Debbie strokes his brow. "Foof!" he sez. "Dat feels nice!"

MEAT CEREMONY

This skull collection---a rawborn chukka.
I wear smears of mud and blood. Sacrificial animals
with lips stretched back and eyes explosive
in amazement at you in the clearing
walking on fire, greased for ancient innovation.
What is about to happen to us?

HER VISION OF THE CAUSE

She eats
        (her body, given for thee)
                                her speed
and all night, red-eyed,
is vigilant.
Because Biafrans starved by the millions?

Or because the dull throb
of unmagnified Berwyn
must experience at least the drama
of Christ afraid for his life
and rapping non-stop to his muse?
He sweats blood
but pops his spirit-boost in and goes on,
awake, but unable
to fully swallow heaven:
"God, will I die?"

Only a red-eyed carpenter
that night on Gethsemane
was sweating.

She has his eyes.

Is it only the drama that leads her that far?
Or is it the weight
of the only-a-carpenter vigilance
that magnifies her through
the Berwyn night?

Sweating blood is no mean feat.

SOLDIER

While he can still hope, he may as well hope
he is hidden. He must think black
in the swamp's black patches, gray where it's gray,
brown, green, invisible. He must try to be
what it is, structure his breathing to be no breathing
but the swamp's. He must move only
like the suck of mud. "There is no soldier
here," he thinks. "This is the swamp."

But he snaps a twig. Or a twig snaps itself---
there is no difference. And enemy forces
see a soldier and mud as separate.
"*There he is!*" they shoot. The target,
so recently trying to act mud, shoots back
to trying to play the role of soldier,
but there is a painful intermission
and a penetration of him by more than bullets.

"*MAMA!*" screams the target
who thought he was mud,
who thought he was a soldier,
who hears the strange voice of whatever he is
and shudders at feeling how little time
there is to learn who is dying here.
The intermission grows long.
The soldier does not return.

FLUTES

Rather the music, a wisp of spirit
than lumbering flesh, its needs

to make, leg-weary through the heat-blasted city
the last filthy bus. Eddie pushes
a wet load of clothes to his place.
He fixes the sink. Good thing there's a parts store!
But tougher every day to repair, to replace
is Eddie. What a man! The salt,
the bread, the stringy meat . . . What a meal!
Was it for this we fought a war
and Lou did not come back?
What a state!

Rather cool extraction, irrelevance
that opens possibility, drifts.

All the free buses that emerge from this cloud
are powder blue
and fan from a hinge.
Shall Eddie go to Haven or Largo or Lee
before coasting home?
Did he wonder if it mattered
that smoky afternoon
long ago
in the dream
she told him about?

Flutes.

The silvery hollow birds
metamorphose --- bamboo,
now clay, they coo a gliss
in his spine and float
into bottomless green.

"Darling, there was everywhere---
in my blood, in the rain---
an avian flutter-tonguing,
and I heard nothing
but that, nor wished to."

THE LIFE OF THE MIND UNDERGROUND

The bat-kissed bones this side of the squeeze
tell the real fat man he need not know
what lies or truth beyond in narrows.
Were there light at this point, Tubby's shadow could go,
for its bulk is specialized---only the fat
that shadows can be---good for doing what whole men cannot.

THAW

Under the white crustacean, she
was cast as a corpse.
Barbed everywhere.
And I, without blood,
was held as fast
in that polar season I frequently prolong.

But, heavenly cycle! Its migration to the sea,
the sky, the big body
began. O, slowly!

And there she was---the medium
in which fat pink earthworms
turn arteries home.
The medium brown in which black in which red
in which water, light, air, exotic sugars green
and move their moving art.
And there she was, naked! I scooped handfuls of
that luscious stuff,
packed an effigy and kissed her astounding,
succulent crotch.
Scoop, pack, and kiss! Song of release!

The air at this adventure was full of chromosomes
and someone remembered the Maypole dance
and the coupling of animals wet the landscapes of home.
My eyes rolled ecstatic
up under the dress
of the sky to the source
of infinite future births.

But then, I remembered

brittle frost returning
first to my bones

and then to my groin
and then merely shrugging off
mushy salute.

I am the ice.

But I was all there
and not ice that time
on the seed in the sky
in the mud goddess then.

ANCESTRAL RESPIRATION

No one's in the hall of the lodge at this moment.
Perhaps they're all stowed in borrowed wombs.
Without them, the fire has slid down the grate
to cast its only light on the spirit of bear grease,
the hands that once hewed these giant black timbers,
and the owls in my bones, my dusty eyes.

ONCOMING TRAFFIC HAS LONGER GREEN

Hello! said America to the young white man.
  The nation was then wearing mini-skirts,
    placement service and a chance for advancement;
    wearing those shoes
    that gave its walk an attractive wiggle
    and slowed its pace to make his trot look good.
Resources--- manpower, raw materials,
    frontier horizons and a wagonload of pork!
  Down the street in lights was O-O-Oak! lahoma.
Well, fancy is as fancy does,
    and fancy did, and didn't he ramble!

Then he's put up behind butcher-paper curtains
    and a cold-water shave next to Nelson Algren,
    in glorified oblivion, once a year displayed
    as perverse or a relic or an object lesson.
He awoke as a tree drawn by pre-school vision---
    not so much a tree as a balanced log
    with a circle for a crown, waiting to topple.
He tossed a few mildewed books in the Volkswagen,
    a family portrait with an angry red X,
    the cold soup of hopes and the mockery of some shoetrees.
And, of course, the ever-slimmer selection of want-ads,
    the yellowing scraps of his paper credentials,
    phone numbers, skyhooks, a rabbit's foot,
And, strangest cargo, a dawning awareness of
    the simultaneity of experience:

Even as he slunk away from childhood sweetheart,
    blender and boatwax,
    with only the chance that J. Paul Getty
    never had --- the chance to start again
    without a goddam seed except his wits, o, so atrophied ---
Even as he madly erased his self-image,
    a hoodlum dozed in remedial reading.

The ground crew snapped the last Boeing buckle,
an African succumbed and a lottery winner.
Asparagus grew many inches
and the lawn-care manual went to press.

Somewhere a version of Scott and Zelda crashing
flickered again to unknown purpose:
"Let's have a drink and enjoy the Riviera,"
and, "Where did I go wrong?"
asks the soiled nostalgia buff.

The image reflected in the skating pond,
gliding and bundled, trailing calligraphy,
later hanging the scarf that's wet with thawed breathfrost
next to the shower curtain, hot cocoa fireside,
Is so intimately related to, soon to be acquainted with
one grotesque blue mammal clawing
at the underside of the saber-toothed glass.
That star in the sky is a hole in the ice.

FRIENDLESS

More hardtack will kill this calloused dream.
Now I must find the wild berries,
for my provisions, given by me
and as given as dust,
are old adventure. Old!
A dot of red or purple
must reopen the frontier;
must pass, sweet or bitter,
through my drying head.

EYES THE RIGHT SIZE

That I looked like Liz Taylor
once can be a touchstone,
millstone or mere stone
to finger,
weigh,
let wear down.

Once, I left home.
Now we snuggle face
to face and luggage.
Life is not over
and above art.
Artfully I sink
my teeth into it
and it gives up
recidivist sighs:
despair, ennui,
contentment.

I will always leave home
and leave home and get here.
Again and again.
I am built for gray joys
like the ones I mentioned.

PARALLAX

I. Predawn

First got in place are the divers lifetimes:
setscrew people, well-fed on theory
and a third generation to fasten it all down.
The salt flat has similarly inched toward this
till it's good for nothing else. A lizard
darts for safety, the most peripheral rock.
The bullet, though, pulls on his fireproof suit
and presses his forehead as he walks to the cannon.
The heart's clock growls on the east horizon.

II. Rocket sled

Instantaneous multi-Gs and my face peels back like a
pink magazine, a surgeon's model, a museum skull.
I must get my whole pelvis into her or
this flat-out scream won't stop at the end.
Life is long or short, this organism wonders.
Was that my all? One stretch on the cross
and smaller now in heaven? My air! thinks Jesus,
What a feeler I was! What a feeler I am,
despite this barren landscape!

III. Debriefing

The antennae of the insects   touch   touch   touch
the spent human fuse   that has fallen to earth.
No meaning.   No meaning.   Is he a typewriter?
Tiny pianists,   skeletal and curious,   hunt and
peck no music.   They watch him learn to place
his feet on the planet.   What does this wobble
mean?   Whence his drool?   But the flatness of
the flat on which analysts reside, the subject's
mad account of the brevity of peak and wrenching
deceleration . . .

MECHANISMS OF FAME

(1)

Not in tried footprints of mom or dad
does he step into the spotlight
nor with their voice say common sense.
There's a funny note on common,
and just as well in his uncommon world.
In space, outside the law,
in his most private moments,
a cold vacuum

for others to fill with their dreams.
His visage! Tonight! His tall name rolls
across the belly of a dirigible,
which comes out of profits.
Down center, he flashes hypnotic teeth---
expensive teeth the masses will pay for,
will pray to, his dentist assured him.
But he has forgotten the dentist, the masses, the planet.

(2)

The 10-foot poster invites a groundling
to come up in the ethers (and she's *seen* the movie).
As soon as she's laid, the chicken crosses the road.
Soon the road is a wide cotton panel
red with guts and fur, feathers and bone.
Exposed in this form, all animal life
is famous, all right, but how *black* it gets in the piney night
till a driver kicks the brights on,

then blindness.
Perhaps she has a premonition
and is puking in fear as she enters the glistening
limousine. No oxygen there.

In the same mirror *he* sees his raison d'etre,
she watches the Minnesota egg farm shrink.
From now on Olaf will be played by Hardy Kruger
and nostalgia be obtained by taking this drug.

(3)

The old story *can* twist. John Lennon decides
he'd rather be human. More in shadow.
And out of the shadows steps a lethal pismire:
"Jodie, I love you. Marilyn is dead."
Soon the sky is a closed frontier,
black with factory jobs and godlessness.
The golden separation between us and them
is illegible now. The giftwrap stinks.

And *still* the organisms that cannot die unknown
rush to take the first of their many meetings,
commission glossies, attend to those details
that would bore a janitor, that would build a myth.
As we speak, they are sitting near their phones,
spending food money on pedicures.
Hometowns don't work alone to kill giants.
All of us arrive at our destinations.

FOLLOW AT A DISTANCE

Our craft, intuition, and visions permit us
aberrations.
There goes Berryman off the bridge.

We coin words like "difficultivate"
and act on them.
There goes Plath into the oven.

On the way to the pub, Dylan Thomas and I
agreed it's tragic
that simple folks simplify themselves to death.

"It's a blackbird," they say.
"Why dwell on it?"
The careful explanation of why, is a poem.

WHAT WE THINK IS MIRACULOUS

The swami escapes,
amphibian through the reed of our faith.
Beyond distance, he surfaces,
bouncing his song above the clouds
and down dark stairs.
It thrives in fog,
on soft ground, in our need.
We would sift the bog, but our bulbs
lose wattage.
As objects fuzz, the swami returns
to whisper at our bedsides, "Miracles!"

SUICIDE NOTE

Thoroughly one (this one) can die.
I can open my hand and let the feathers
scatter in the mystery,
become invisible and sleep through work,
cause unmet demands to accumulate no further
and artifacts loved and unloved to fade.

Whether one imagines an aftermath
of weeping kin unable to reorganize,
the merest vacancy of a tongue-felt hole
where a fresh-yanked tooth has broken a habit,
or only a strangeness
like the memory of a smell,

that ability's a piece of
the omnipresent cipher.
I have broken this much:
I can write it! I can write it.
Strange. Even to *have* a real hand.
What is that language whole?

PEACETIME

Peacetime. Snakes born now
aren't yet aware of
poison's use, brief mercy! Not sensing
the death in
their
sacs.
Snugly nesting in fading memorial days,
not dreaming they'll lurch from sleep
to writhe on the map as forebears did,
trusting themselves
through these, the last of
their prewar days.

"So long ago, it wasn't us," old vipers wish,
"or not our fault," their glands now slack.
As proof, they offer rusty pushpins,
golf with retired profiteers.
Orphans enter trade schools.
Diplomats visit eroding craters,
dropping late, half-hearted semi-confession.
But the hiss forks home to Vinegar Seep
and plans for new foes:
The damn recurring dream
of why and what and where and how
and bloody who!

"Forget all that snake business, fuggin poet!
Snake is meat and I eat meat
and here's the knife I stick it with!"
... and speaks English, stands erect,
exhibits affection for those of its kind
and punches you inna mout if you say
there weren't any good old days
of two-bit haircuts, nickel cuppa joe.
And works as hard as any two men

to drum from his veteran stump the memories:
Shattered reach, old bundles of touch.
"Don't mope around *this* peacetime, Mac!"

Heal like that stump---
without long bone
as long as it's gone.
Where this species once might have projected,
curl in at the edge of
the ongoing wound
of what your serpent heart contains
and call that healing.
It's peacetime. Memorial Day as well.
Take the day of vacation offered
to shed as much skin
as luck, brief mercy, allows.

HEAT

We were to grill the suspect
all night if necessary
to discover . . .? I forget.
I remember pondering
the meaning of the word "grill."
97-degree heat
without a breeze, close quarters,
and hateful duty combined
to blur my thoughts: Grilled like meat?
Like a face pressed against bars?
Will these questions never end?

HOSPICE

I am here now this way,
like Count Korzybski
and the other animals---
bodily mess and a painful load
of something cerebral,
going up and down
and trying to relax
in friend and relative comfort,
but aspiring, second guessing,
and envisioning the future,
one part per millions.
The suspense is killing me.

Liquids come and go,
container-shaped.
Participation should be easy:
Go outdoors, where nature is,
and act in accordance
with what I am.
Can I do otherwise?
A painful load of something
abstract: a 12-line stanza
and high ideals, but
I want to go indoors.
I want to sleep with you.

Shall I be frank?
If I am not frank,
you'll never know me, love.
If I love you, love,
I will want you to know,
but not know pain,
but I'll pain you, love,
if I am frank.
I may roll in my sleep

and crush you, love.
I will eat you if I'm hungry
and snarl if I'm scared.

I will smell like an animal
before the end. How much will does it take
to conceal such failures?
How much will not to share
malignant oranges
when I want to share everything
in this cage?
It is all I have---
ungodly howls
are an apt description.
And how are you? asks a saint.

MIRROR IN PUBLIC

Here is a portentious eye. I turn away
to face a second asymmetry and turn again.
Today, every passenger seems a freak
and I turn away, turn away, intestines shriveling
and turn away from my turning away.
A poison tide is lifting my flimsy boat.

SPATTERED BLOOD IN FIVE PASTELS

The high cost of flying, the higher cost of staying
with smiles or grimaces where we are
incomplete. Strip-mine
this park!

Fold it in sixteenths and stick it in the glovebox!
Kansas, Nebraska, Utah must be destroyed
and the dollhouse furniture of maptalk
that mocks our stretchmarks:

semicircles where drumlins are,
tees where tungsten can be got.
And here, Confederates struggled to prove
that a nation divided makes some kind of sense.

Her map, my map---striated by 2,000 miles
of nervous roads and rails, wires and postal routes.
Deepest reds and blues lacerate the phony calm
of five pastels. The unity needs a fix.

In which of those veins may we inject ourselves?
In the desert? On the prairie?
In which capital or backwash
drive the golden spike and long endure?

BLACK SKY BLUES

We are passing over The City of Brotherly Love
and clouds and clouds no feeling penetrates.
The pilot says we are flying high.
Farmers' problems are now abstract designs.

The flight attendant has painted on her head
a helpful face to show how the mask goes on
and instructs us to continue breathing normally.
She brings a sealed bag of cold utensils.

Would I care to wire home a thoughtful gift?
What thought? What home? I'd care for a pillow,
for eternal suspension above those clouds
and the messy history of me on the ground.

I'm best at droning toward a servile inn
and someone else's business, good on paper
cups of coffee, plastic cups of booze,
peaceful in a rented car with a borrowed map.

I'm a pioneer of nothingness,
come into thin air and lounge apart
from a distant planet. I call
with a button: "Plug me into muzak."

THE EGG OF WHO YOU ARE NOW OPENED

Now you say it was bitter-sweet.
I'm not sure I know what you mean.
That Christmas morning long ago,
when the egg of who you are now opened
the year's last package and said Oh, no!
The center of the universe is not here!
It's the wrong model, wrong size, I am dead!

Why? Why? Why?
You had asked them, you had told them,
and you *had* been good,
so why did they kill you
with something *other*?

You did not make yourself clear.
You *do* not make yourself clear.
The important things
cannot be made clear.
You may as well begin thinking
of Christmas Future as bitter-sweet.
That is relatively clear.

WHERE TO BEGIN

Does one begin with a palm-sized scrap
broken arbitrarily from the rest
or must the puzzle solve all at once?

Skydivers favor a headlong plunge.
Scholars on the other hand.
Everyone suffers and celebrates

chosen bindings of skin or page
or icon or drug or expertise
or art or idea or fad or fury,

environment, heredity, cosmetic devices,
changes of address and not enough money,
a muscle tear, a dropped fly ball,

the Martians, who may already be among us,
what my idiot uncle said,
fear of four more years of Republicans.

Ways are The Way (and the grain embargo)---
any, all, one, another (How 'bout them Bears?)
The poly-amorphous subject IS

and denial of it, too. It irrefutes itself
as the goal. Even as it distances.
One begins with whatever one can catch first.

LEGACY WEATHER

To the sky for his children he pointed: "There's the proof.
Wherever we are there are areas such as these,"
he said, pointing to his head,
cumulonimbus, they sensed even then.
A generation later, his thunder echoed,
exquisitely changed to a similar truth.